Paralympics

By Mike Artell

DOMINIE PRESS
Pearson Learning Group

Publisher: Raymond Yuen
Project Editor: John S. F. Graham
Editor: Bob Rowland
Designer: Greg DiGenti
Photographs: Reuters New Media/Corbis (Cover/Page 14);
Bettmann/Corbis (page 6); AFP/Corbis (pages 11 and 17);
Richard T. Nowitz/Corbis (Page 21)

Paralympic logo courtesy of the International Paralympic
Committee

Published by:

🐾 Dominie Press, Inc.

1949 Kellogg Avenue
Carlsbad, California 92008 USA

www.dominie.com

1-800-232-4570

Paperback ISBN 0-7685-1835-0
Printed in Singapore
 5 6   10 09 08 07 06

Table of Contents

Chapter One

The History of the Paralympic Games

In 1944, the world was at war. Many soldiers were badly hurt and would never walk again.

In England, there was a special hospital for soldiers with disabling back injuries. It was called Stoke Mandeville.

The doctors at this hospital were very good at helping soldiers learn how to live with their disabilities.

A doctor named Sir Ludwig Guttman worked at the Stoke Mandeville hospital for veterans of World War II. Dr. Guttman believed that playing sports would help

Wheelchair javelin thrower Joep de Beer of the Netherlands in the Stoke Mandeville Games of 1954— Dr. Guttman is the man on the left in glasses

the veterans stay healthy both physically and mentally. He reasoned that the veterans could play sports, even though they were in wheelchairs and had disabilities.

Dr. Guttman encouraged the soldiers to have wheelchair races and to play other games, like javelin throwing and basketball. The soldiers found out that playing sports helped them to stay strong. They gradually realized that they could still do things that other people did, despite their disabilities.

In 1948, the veterans at Stoke Mandeville challenged other hospitals around England to a sports competition. They called the competition the Stoke Mandeville Games.

A few years later, in 1952, veterans from hospitals in the Netherlands joined the games. It was now a truly international competition.

In 1960, the games were held in Rome and the name was changed from the Stoke Mandeville Games to the Paralympics. Some of the original sports at the first Paralympics were fencing, basketball, table tennis, javelin throwing, snooker pool, shot put, swimming, and archery. Four hundred athletes from twenty-three countries participated.

In 1976, the Paralympics introduced the Winter Games, hosted by Sweden. They featured only a few events, such as downhill skiing. Later, as the Winter Games became more popular, more events were added, such as sit-skiing, biathlon, and ice sledge hockey.

Chapter Two
The Modern Paralympic Games

Today, the Paralympic Games make up the world's second-largest sporting event. They are held every four years, just like the Olympic Games.

Since 1988, the Olympic athletes and the Paralympic athletes have had their games in the same city. The Paralympic Games take place two weeks after the Olympic Games are over.

A flame is kept burning while the Paralympic Games are being played. Runners take turns carrying the torch that lights the flame, which is lit during a ceremony at the beginning of the games.

The three shapes on the Paralympic logo represent the organization's motto: Mind, Body, and Spirit. The colors used on the logo—green, red, and blue—were chosen because many countries have those three colors on their flags.

During the Sydney, Australia Summer Paralympic Games in 2000, more than 3,800 athletes from 123 countries competed. Over 500 athletes from 40 countries participated in the 2002 Winter Paralympic Games in Salt Lake City, Utah.

Norway plays the U.S.A. in the Gold Medal game of ice sledge hockey at the 2002 Paralympic games in Salt Lake City, Utah

The sports of the Winter Paralympic Games are:

- Alpine skiing
- Cross-country skiing
- Ice sledge hockey
- Biathlon

The sports of the Summer Paralympic Games are:

- Archery
- Shooting
- Athletics
- Swimming
- Basketball
- Table Tennis
- Cycling
- Tennis
- Equestrian
- Volleyball
- Fencing
- Boccia
- Football
- Goalball
- Judo
- Powerlifting
- Sailing
- Rugby

Chapter Three
The Athletes

There are many different kinds of Paralympic events. In the blind judo competition, blind athletes are judged by the same rules that govern the Olympic Games.

Other competitions have different

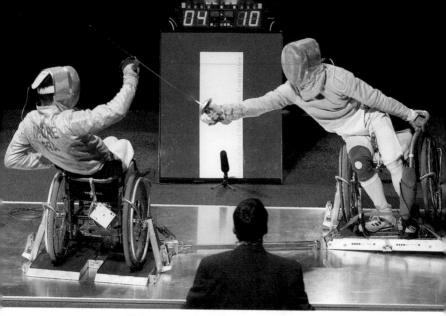
**Chinese fencing champion Fung Ying-ki
lunges at French fencer Cyril Moore**

rules for Paralympic versions of the
sports. For example, in ice sledge hockey,
players sit on a kind of two-bladed sled
and control the puck with two short
sticks instead of one long one.

In wheelchair fencing, the wheelchairs
are held in one place on the floor.
Scoring is the same as for Olympic
fencing, but the competitors must follow
strict rules about moving in their chairs.

Fung Ying-ki is a Chinese wheelchair fencing champion. He permanently lost the use of his legs when he was thirteen because of a rare virus. When he was fifteen, he decided to try fencing from his wheelchair and found that he had a talent for it. By the time he was twenty, he had won the Paralympic gold medal.

Blind skiers race down the hills with the help of guides. On the sidelines, these guides talk to the athletes over loudspeakers while they are skiing to let them know which way to turn. Skiers who do not have two legs can use one ski. They balance themselves with ski crutches.

Sarah Billmeier is a Paralympic skier from Maine. When she was five years old, she lost her left leg from above the knee to bone cancer. She started skiing when she was eight. In 1992, at the age of fourteen, she won two gold medals in downhill skiing at the Winter Paralympic Games in Albertville, France. Since then, competing in three different Paralympic Games, she won seven additional gold medals, five silvers, and a bronze, including a gold and silver at Salt Lake City in 2002. She has also won six world skiing titles outside the Paralympics.

Zanele Situ is from South Africa. She is a wheelchair athlete and champion javelin thrower. At the 2000 games in Sydney, Australia, she became the first black woman to win a Paralympic gold medal.

Marlon Shirley is a runner from the United States who holds the world Paralympic record for the 100-meter race. He ran that race in 11.08 seconds in the 2000 Sydney Games and won

U.S. Paralympic runner Marlon Shirley

the gold medal. The world record for non-Paralympic athletes is 9.78 seconds. He also won the silver medal in the high jump competition.

Marlon holds a number of Paralympic track and field records, including the 60-meter sprint, the high jump, and the long jump.

He was in a lawn-mower accident when he was five years old and lost his leg below the knee. He wears a special prosthetic device to allow him to compete in sprint races as well as other track and field events. The device acts like a foot and has a special spring action similar to that of an ankle.

During the 1998 games, Miyuki Kobayashi won the first Paralympic gold medal for Japan. Miyuki, who is blind, competed in the biathlon. The biathlon is an event that combines skiing and shooting.

Cheri Becerra-Madsen (cover photo) is a Native American wheelchair racer from the United States. One morning, when she was four years old, she woke up unable to use her legs. A condition known as transverse myelitis paralyzed her legs, making her unable to walk. But she was always a very active child and developed her arm strength by swimming and pushing her wheelchair as fast as it could go.

She decided to become a world-class wheelchair racer at 18 when she read about the sport in a magazine. At the 1996 Paralympic Games, she won two silver medals and two bronze. At the 2000 games, she won three gold medals and a silver, including a world-record setting time in the 100-meter sprint.

Wheelchair basketball is one of the most popular team sports at the Paralympic Games. The athletes play on the same court and use the same baskets as running basketball players.

Some rules are different because the players move differently in wheelchairs. For example, to dribble the ball, the player must bounce it at least once between two "pushes" on the wheels of the chair.

The Canadian Men's Wheelchair Basketball team won the gold medal at the 2000 Paralympic Games. The Canadian Women's Wheelchair Basketball team also won the gold medal in 2000, their third in a row.

Chapter Four

Sports Equipment for Disabled Athletes

Many companies make equipment for athletes with disabilities. They have equipment for beginners and experienced athletes, too.

Some of the special equipment the Paralympic athletes use costs thousands

There are many companies that make
sports equipment for disabled children and adults

of dollars. It is too expensive for many of
them to buy, so they get sponsors to help
pay for the equipment.

Organizations for Disabled Athletes

Many of the athletes in the Paralympic
Games train at the National Sports

Center for the Disabled in Winter Park, Colorado.

This organization provides sports training for both the summer and winter Paralympic athletes.

They even have programs for families with disabled children who just want to have fun.

The Paralyzed Veterans of America is another group that offers sports programs for disabled athletes.

It takes courage to compete in any sport or activity. Paralympic athletes teach us that nothing can keep someone from going for the gold if that person has the heart of a champion.

Would You Like to Know More?

There are many Internet web sites with information about the Paralympics. Just do a search on the word *Paralympics*.

Your library may also have books about the Paralympic athletes or other disabled athletes. Sometimes sports magazines feature articles about disabled athletes.